EASY ORIGAMI

Ocean Animals

An Augmented Reading Paper Folding Experience

BY
JOHN MONTROLL

CAPSTONE PRESS
a capstone imprint

TABLE OF CONTENTS

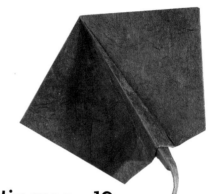

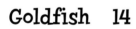

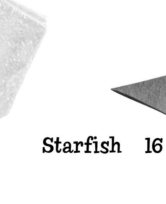

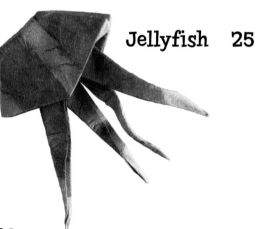

ORIGAMI OCEAN ADVENTURE

Dive into an ocean of origami! On this amazing paper-folding adventure, you'll fold tropical fish, sharks, jellyfish, squid, and so much more.

Best of all, every model in this book is easy to fold. Simple instructions and diagrams walk you through every step. And if you get stuck, just watch the Capstone 4D videos. They'll show you each fold in action.

So grab some paper squares and flex your fingers. Your favorite ocean animals are just a few folds away!

Download the Capstone app!

- Ask an adult to download the Capstone 4D app.

- Scan the cover and stars inside the book for additional content.

When you scan a spread, you'll find fun extra stuff to go with this book! You can also find these things on the web at www.capstone4D.com using the password: ocean.13073

SYMBOLS

Lines

_ _ _ _ _ _ _ _ _   Valley fold, fold in front.

_ · · _ · · _ · · _ · · _   Mountain fold, fold behind.

———————   Crease line.

····················   X-ray or guide line.

Arrows

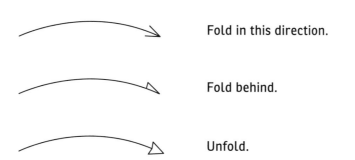

Fold in this direction.

Fold behind.

Unfold.

Fold and unfold.

Turn over.

Sink or three dimensional folding.

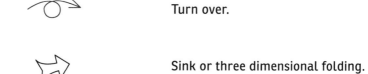

Place your finger between these layers.

BASIC FOLDS ★

Pleat Fold

Fold back and forth. Each pleat is composed of one valley and mountain fold. Here are two examples.

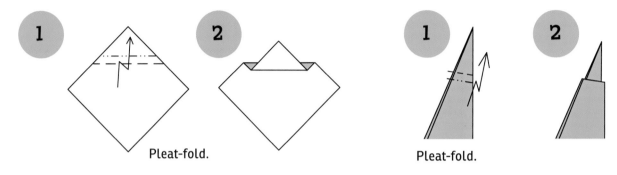

1 **2** Pleat-fold.

1 **2** Pleat-fold.

Squash Fold

In a squash fold, some paper is opened and then made flat. The shaded arrow shows where to place your finger.

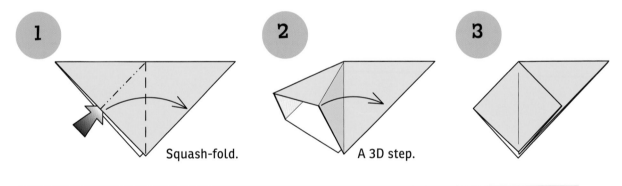

1 Squash-fold. **2** A 3D step. **3**

Rabbit Ear

To fold a rabbit ear, one corner is folded in half and laid down to a side.

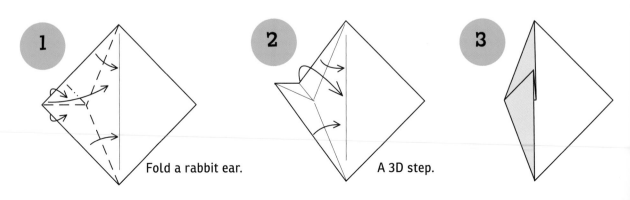

1 Fold a rabbit ear. **2** A 3D step. **3**

Inside Reverse Fold

In an inside reverse fold, some paper is folded between layers. Here are two examples.

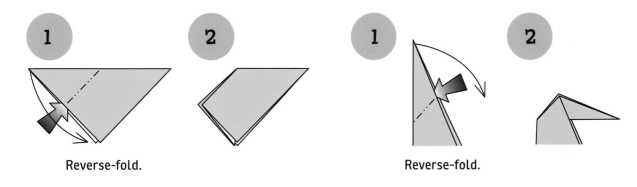

Reverse-fold.

Reverse-fold.

Outside Reverse Fold

Much of the paper must be unfolded to make an outside reverse fold.

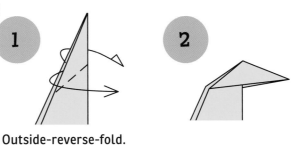

Outside-reverse-fold.

Crimp Fold

A crimp fold is a combination of two reverse folds. Open the model slightly to form the crimp evenly on each side. Here are two examples.

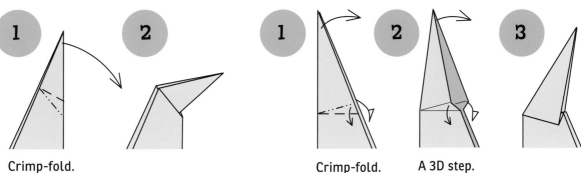

Crimp-fold.

Crimp-fold.

A 3D step.

TROPICAL FISH

Flitting through the waters blue
Are tropical fish in rainbow hues.
Some sport yellow, blue, and red—
Others wear thin stripes instead.
How do they learn to look so cool?
No doubt by swimming in their schools.

1

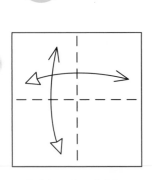

Fold and unfold.
Rotate the model.

2

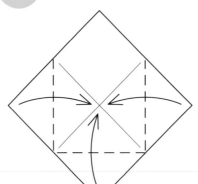

Fold three corners
to the center.

3

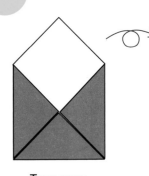

Turn over.

8

4

Fold and unfold.
Turn over.

5

Collapse along
the creases.

6

A 3D step.

7

Fold the top layer down
so the dots meet.

8

This is 3D. Flatten.

9

Turn over and
rotate the model.

10

Tropical Fish

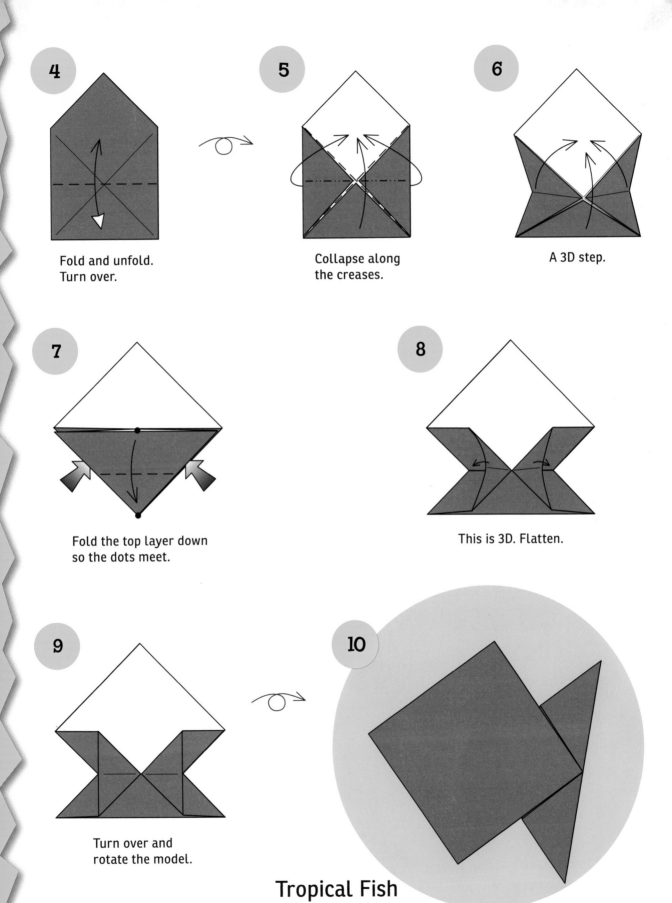

9

STINGRAY

All throughout the coral reef
Swim strange creatures beyond belief.
Flat and wide, these stingrays glide,
And often in the sand they hide.
But watch out for their long, thin tails
With hidden stingers as sharp as nails.

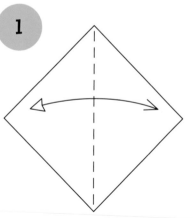

1

Fold and unfold.

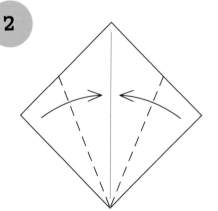

2

Fold to the center.

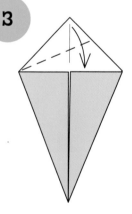

3

Fold down.

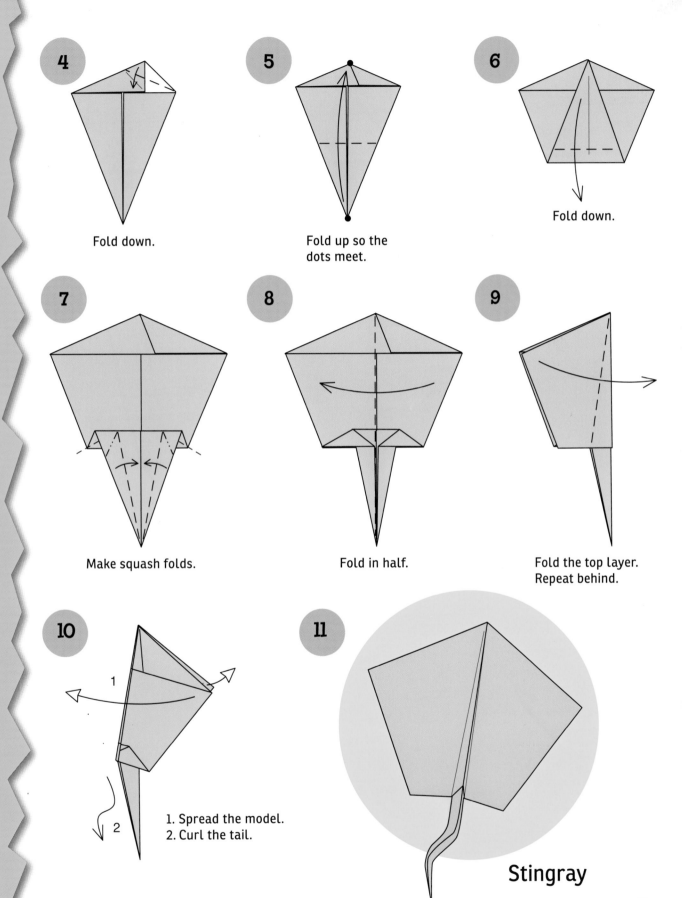

4

Fold down.

5

Fold up so the
dots meet.

6

Fold down.

7

Make squash folds.

8

Fold in half.

9

Fold the top layer.
Repeat behind.

10

1
2

1. Spread the model.
2. Curl the tail.

11

Stingray

EEL

Eels do not need fancy fins
To cut the water as they swim.
Just like ribbons in a breeze,
Their bodies wave with gentle ease.
And if they need a course correction,
They quick reverse their wave direction.

1

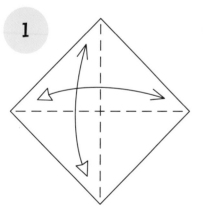

Fold and unfold.

2

Fold to the center.

3

Fold to the center.

4

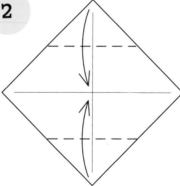

Valley-fold so
the dots meet.

5

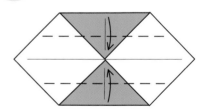

Fold in half.

12

6

Valley-fold.

7

Unfold.

8

Reverse-fold along the crease.

9

Fold up and repeat behind.

10

1
i 2

1. Fold the eye down, repeat behind.
2. Reverse-fold the mouth.

11

Shape the eel.

12

Eel

GOLDFISH

If you're looking for a bold fish,
Look no further than a goldfish.
In the sun's bright, gleaming glimmer,
You'll find no fear in this brave swimmer.
He glitters golden without care
Like no other fish would ever dare.

1

Fold in half.

2

Fold in half.

3

Fold up and
repeat behind.

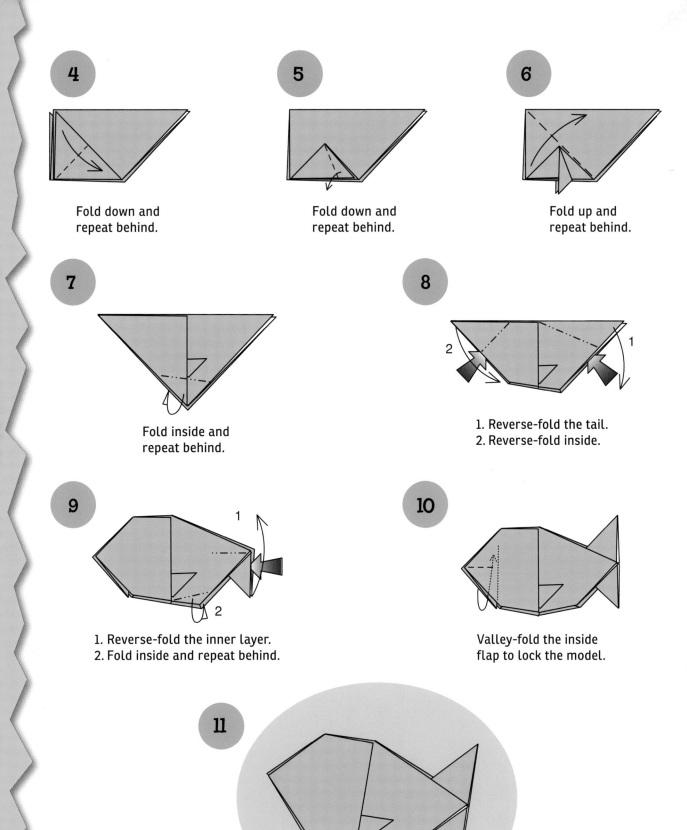

4 Fold down and repeat behind.

5 Fold down and repeat behind.

6 Fold up and repeat behind.

7 Fold inside and repeat behind.

8
1. Reverse-fold the tail.
2. Reverse-fold inside.

9
1. Reverse-fold the inner layer.
2. Fold inside and repeat behind.

10 Valley-fold the inside flap to lock the model.

11

Goldfish

STARFISH

A common starfish has its charms,
Though none compare to its five arms.
It uses them to slowly creep
And pick up tasty treats to eat.
But best of all, if it's attacked,
The limbs it loses will grow back.

1

Fold in half.

2

Fold down.

3

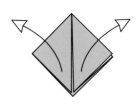

Unfold.

4

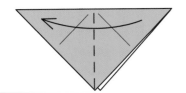

Fold in half.

5

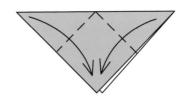

Fold the dot to
the bold line.

6

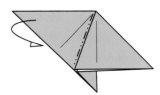

Fold behind.

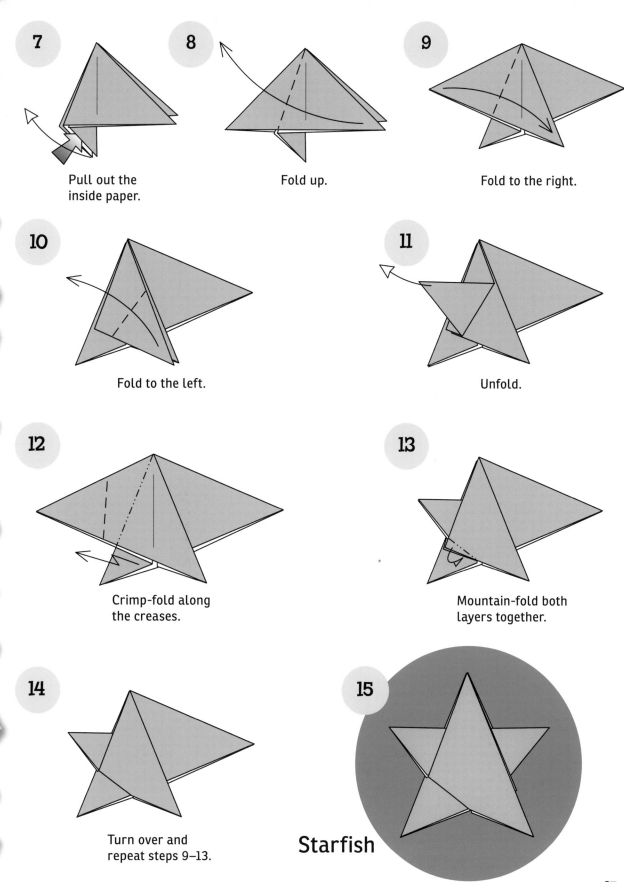

7 Pull out the inside paper.

8 Fold up.

9 Fold to the right.

10 Fold to the left.

11 Unfold.

12 Crimp-fold along the creases.

13 Mountain-fold both layers together.

14 Turn over and repeat steps 9–13.

15 Starfish

SCALLOP

A scallop has a pretty shell
That hides its secrets very well.
Its mantle's edge is lined with eyes—
Up to one hundred, to our surprise!
And for a gift fit for an earl,
Look inside for a rare pearl.

1

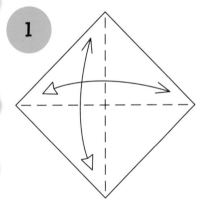

Fold and unfold.

2

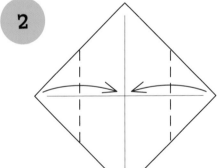

Fold to the center.

3

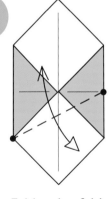

Fold and unfold.

4

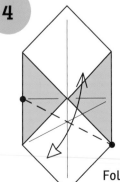

Fold and unfold.
Turn over.

5

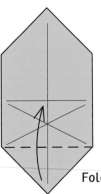

Fold to the center.

6

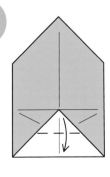

Fold down.

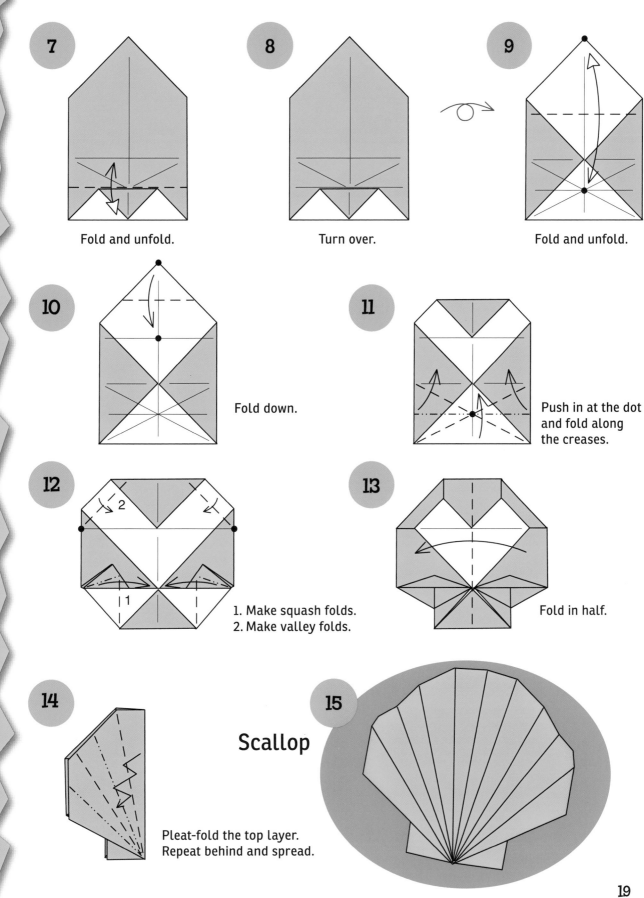

7 Fold and unfold.

8 Turn over.

9 Fold and unfold.

10 Fold down.

11 Push in at the dot and fold along the creases.

12
1. Make squash folds.
2. Make valley folds.

13 Fold in half.

14 Pleat-fold the top layer. Repeat behind and spread.

15

Scallop

SHARK

When you see a dorsal fin,
Don't waste time—just come on in
And trade the water for the beach
Where this hunter cannot reach.
For when a shark is in your sights,
It's best to avoid its pearly whites.

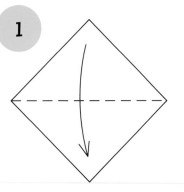

1

Fold in half.

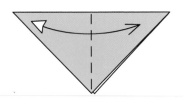

2

Fold and unfold.

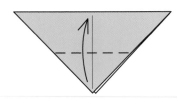

3

Fold the top layer up.

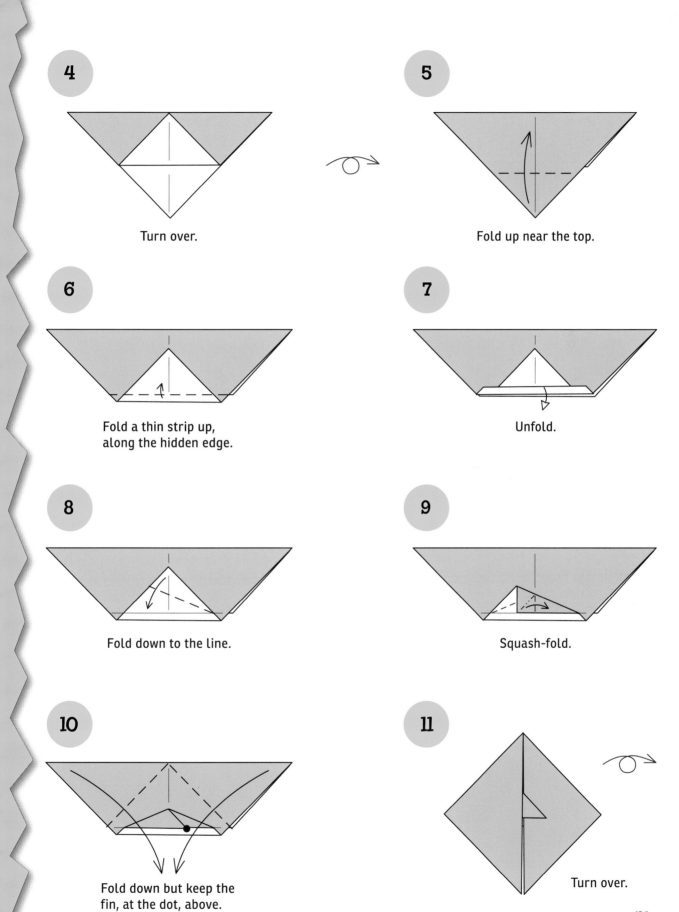

4

Turn over.

5

Fold up near the top.

6

Fold a thin strip up,
along the hidden edge.

7

Unfold.

8

Fold down to the line.

9

Squash-fold.

10

Fold down but keep the
fin, at the dot, above.

11

Turn over.

21

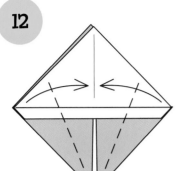

12

Fold to the center.

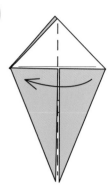

13

Fold and unfold
the top layer.

14

Fold in half and
rotate the model.

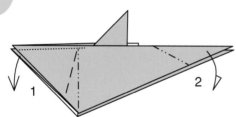

15

1. Crimp-fold the inner layer.
2. Mountain-fold, repeat behind.

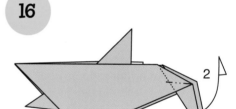

16

1. Fold inside, repeat behind.
2. Mountain-fold one flap up.

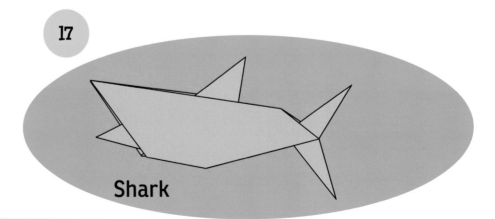

17

Shark

SQUID

The time has come to give a nod
To the remarkable cephalopod.
The squid is king of the deep, blue ocean
When it comes to rapid motion.
It sucks in water and then expels it,
And thus a jet is what propels it.

1

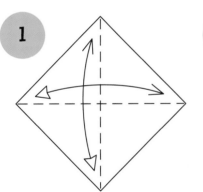

Fold and unfold.

2

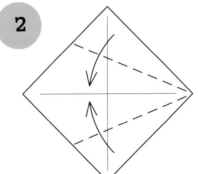

Fold to the center.

3

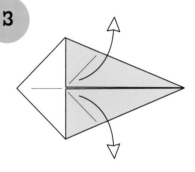

Unfold.

4

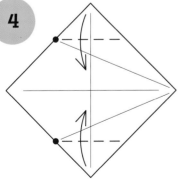

Make valley folds.

5

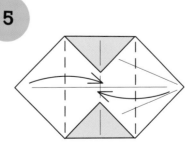

Make valley folds.

6

Unfold.

7 Fold the corners to the dot.

8 Unfold.

9 Valley-fold so the dots meet.

10 Pleat-fold along the creases.

11 Squash-fold to the center.

12 Squash-fold to the center.

13 Fold behind and to the center.

14 Fold to the center and swing out from behind.

15 Turn over.

16 Pleat-fold.

17 Unfold and bend in half very slightly.

18 Squid

JELLYFISH

On the ocean's changing tide,
A jellyfish enjoys the ride.
Drifting where the currents go,
Gliding with the ebb and flow
Like an undersea umbrella—
Oh, what a life for this fine fella!

1

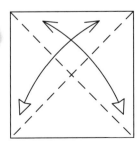

Fold and unfold.

2

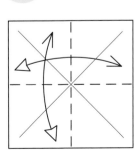

Fold and unfold.

3

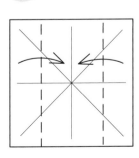

Fold to the center.

25

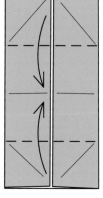

4

Fold to the center.

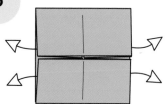

5

Pull out the corners.

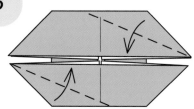

6

Fold opposite edges to the center.

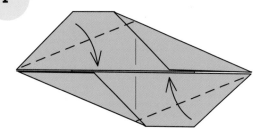

7

Fold opposite edges to the center.

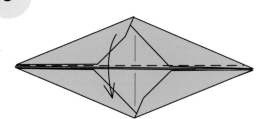

8

Fold in half.

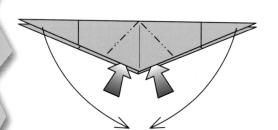

9

Make reverse folds along the creases.

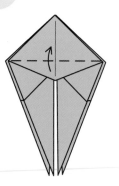

10

Fold up. (Do not repeat behind.)

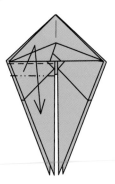

11

Pleat-fold all the layers.

12

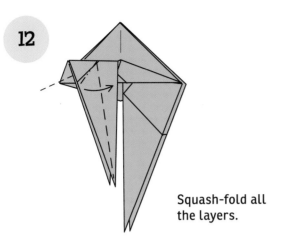

Squash-fold all the layers.

13

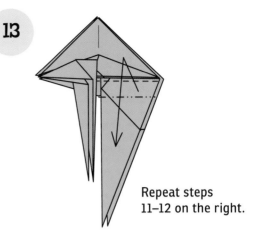

Repeat steps 11–12 on the right.

14

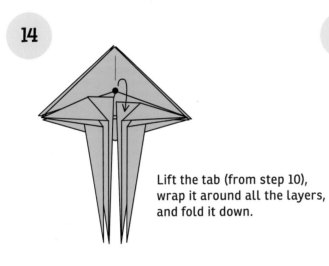

Lift the tab (from step 10), wrap it around all the layers, and fold it down.

15

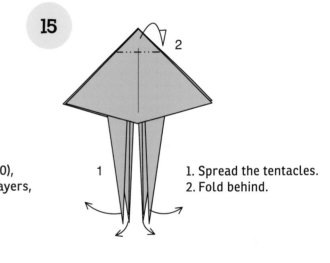

1
2

1. Spread the tentacles.
2. Fold behind.

16

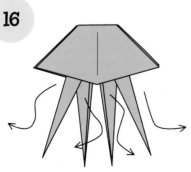

Shape the tentacles by folding, bending, and curling.

17

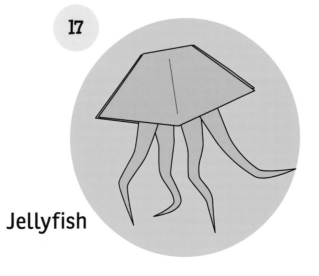

Jellyfish

SEAHORSE

Bobbing through the green seaweed
Bounds the ocean's noble steed.
Pushed along by a dorsal fin,
The seahorse does his best to swim
Until he finds—without fail—
A place to perch his curly tail.

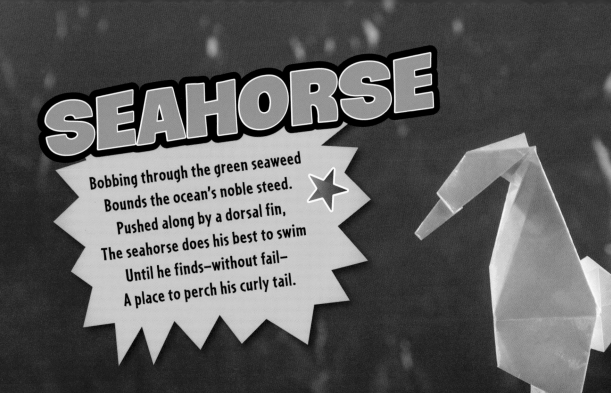

1

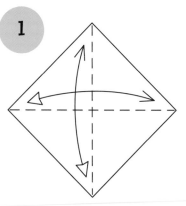

Fold and unfold.

2

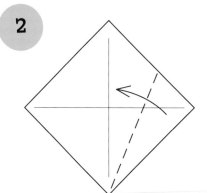

Fold to the center.

3

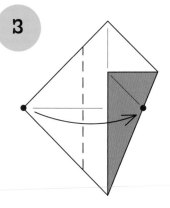

Valley-fold so
the dots meet.

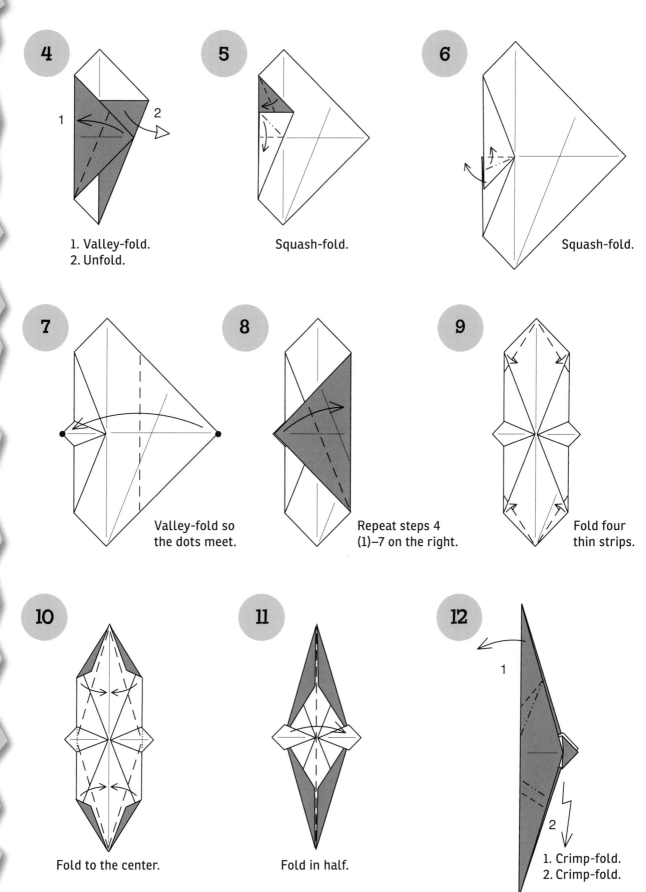

4

1. Valley-fold.
2. Unfold.

5

Squash-fold.

6

Squash-fold.

7

Valley-fold so
the dots meet.

8

Repeat steps 4
(1)–7 on the right.

9

Fold four
thin strips.

10

Fold to the center.

11

Fold in half.

12

1. Crimp-fold.
2. Crimp-fold.

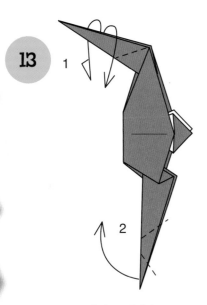

13

1. Crimp-fold.
2. Reverse folds.

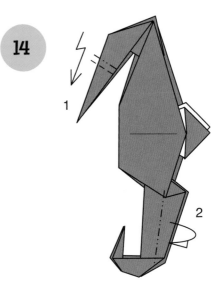

14

1. Crimp-fold.
2. Fold inside, repeat behind.

15

1. Reverse-fold.
2. Fold inside, repeat behind.

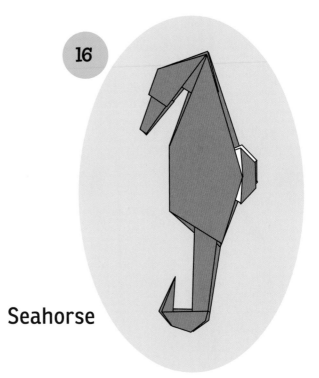

16

Seahorse

Read More

Gardiner, Matthew. *Origami Animals.* New York: Windmill Books, 2016.

Harbo, Christopher. *Easy Origami Ornaments.* Origami Crafting in 4D. North Mankato, Minn.: Capstone Press, 2017.

Hardyman, Robyn. *Ocean Animals.* Origami Fun. Minneapolis: Bellwether Media, Inc., 2018.

Owen, Ruth. *Polar Animals.* Origami Safari. New York: Windmill Books, 2015.

Internet Sites

Use FactHound to find Internet sites related to this book.

Visit *www.facthound.com*

Just type in 9781543513073 and go.

Makerspace Tips

Download tips and tricks for using this book and others in a library makerspace.

Visit www.capstonepub.com/dabblelabresources

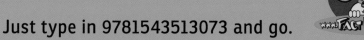

Dabble Lab Books are published by Capstone Press
1710 Roe Crest Drive, North Mankato, Minnesota 56003
www.mycapstone.com

Library of Congress Cataloging-in-Publication Data is
available at the Library of Congress website.
ISBN: 978-1-5435-1307-3 (library binding)
ISBN: 978-1-5435-1311-0 (eBook PDF)

Editorial Credits
Christopher Harbo, editor; Lori Bye, designer;
Morgan Walters, media researcher; Kathy McColley,
production specialist

Photo Credits
Capstone Studio/Karon Dubke, all photos;
John Montroll, all diagrams

Printed and bound in the USA. PA021

John Montroll is respected for his work in origami throughout the
world. He started folding in elementary school and quickly progressed
from folding models from books to creating his own designs. Today,
John has written and published many books, and each origami model
that he designs has a meticulously developed folding sequence. The
American origami master is known for being the inspiration behind
the single-square, no cuts, no glue approach in origami, and his
long-standing experience allows him to accomplish a model in fewer
steps, rather than more. It is John's constant goal to give the reader a
pleasing folding experience.